August 1994

For Larry,
With thanks for all the time,
information and insight you've
so generously shared —

Sheila

The Snake Song

Sheila Farr

*a selection from a series of poems
prompted by Indian miniature paintings,
myths, and stone carvings*

✻ ✻ ✻ ✻ ✻

The Signpost Press Inc
1007 Queen Street
Bellingham, WA 98226

Acknowledgements

Some of the poems in this collection
have appeared in the following publications:

The American Literary Review
Delhi London Poetry Quarterly
Jeopardy
The New York Quarterly
The Quarterly

Reproductions appear
courtesy of the following collections:

Bharat Kala Bhavan, Varanasi
Chandigarh Museum, Chandigarh
Government Museum, Mathura
The National Museum, New Delhi
Sri Pritap Singh Museum, Srinagar
The State Museum, Lucknow
Mr. Vinod Krishna Kanoria

Cover design by Ken Leback

Cover art:
18th c. Pahari miniature (detail)
courtesy of Mr. Vinod Krishna Kanoria

Special thanks to
David Nechak and Stephanie Snyder
for their contributions.

Copyright © 1994 by Sheila Farr
ISBN 0-936563-16-8
Library of Congress Catalog Card Number: 94-65709

Contents

I. Beginnings

Unconscious Acts 11
The Birth of Twilight 12
Oversight 14
Death 15
The Howler 16
Indifference 18
The Milking of Prithvi 19

II. The Great Blue God

The Sari Thief 23
Sporting with the Gopis 26
Krishna's Lament 29
Radha's Bath 31
Painting Radha's Toenails 32

III. Night and the River

The Snake Song 36
Night and the River 39
When Vines Shed Their Leaves 41
Majnun, the Mad One 43
Monsoon 45
The Betrayal 46
The Undoing 47
Emerging from the Beast 49

IV. Legends, Icons, and Endings

The Hermit 53
Weapons of the Gods 55
A Hindu Offering 56
Sohni and the Herdsman 57
The Forest Song 61
Unveiling Draupadi 63
Ganesha 64
A Village Shrine 65
Durga and the Demon 66
She 67

Reproductions

11
18th c. Pahari (detail): State Museum, Lucknow
13
18th c. Pahari (detail): Bharat Kala Bhavan, Varanasi
24
18th c. Pahari (detail): National Museum, New Delhi
28
17th c. Pahari (detail): Sri Pratap Singh Museum, Srinagar
30
19th c. Pahari: collection of the author
35
18th c. Pahari (detail): Vinod Krishna Kanoria
38
18th c. Rajasthan: Chandigarh Museum, Chandigarh
40
17th c. Pahari: Sri Pritap Singh Museum, Srinagar
42
17th c. Mughal: National Museum, New Delhi
44
18th c. Pahari: Bharat Kala Bhavan, Varanasi
47
2nd c. B.C. Sandstone, from Sarnath:
National Museum, New Delhi
48
2nd c. Red sandstone, from Sonkh, Mathura:
Government Museum, Mathura
58
18th c. Pahari: Bharat Kala Bhavan, Varanasi
60
2nd-3rd c. Red sandstone, from Mathura:
Government Museum, Mathura
62
18th c. Pahari: Chandigarh Museum, Chandigarh

The Snake Song

for my friends
...

I.

Beginnings

Unconscious Acts

One day, Brahma grew tired
  of always creating, creating.
Lazily, he stretched back
  to admire his pristine universe.
He yawned.
  And from that passive, fecund void
all hell broke loose:
  a swirling, a coagulate mass
of teeth, horns, tusks, claws,
  of seething and voracious eyes.
Then Brahma slept.
  And in his dark and primal depth
a thousand desperate needs congealed.
  The face of evil emerged.

The Birth of Twilight

As Brahma slept,
a dream shuddered through him:
a lustful dream,
the potent dream of a god;
and a clot of strange desires
spewed from his hidden self,
was born writhing and hissing
to the light.
Loosed like a tangle of snakes,
these depraved demons,
these frenzied asuras
turned with twisted longing
upon their own maker.

Repelled,
Brahma closed his eyes to them.
Harassed,
Brahma rose and ran from them
and beseeched Lord Vishnu,
light of the world,
for advice.

"Assume another form,"
replied the lord of lotus and scepter.
"Appease this ravening horde,"
commanded the flame of knowledge.

Sighing,
Brahma shaped himself
as Sandhya, loveliest of maidens,
stepped, radiant and serene,
before the darkly advancing throng.
Greedily,
the obscene-eyed asuras
appraised the woman's divine form:
her glowing skin, her dusky eyes,
her round hips wrapped
in transparent sunset hues.
Leering,

they pressed about her, seized her,
and, tearing at her sun-tinted silks,
crept off with her.

Now, each evening,
they slink back, ravenous,
to the radiant temple of the gods.
Each evening,
Sandhya is sacrificed anew.

Oversight

Brahma knew he'd made a mistake.
   He looked out over the world:
people and animals stood everywhere
   with no space between them.
And anger burst from him in huge flames
   scorching the earth
and all its creatures.

The gods begged him to stop.
   "This isn't right," they said,
"ruining everything you just made."

So Brahma suppressed his rage.
   And from his eyes, his ears,
his nose and mouth
   the form of a woman emerged:
delicate and dark-eyed,
   dressed in red.

Pleased, Brahma said to himself,
   "She can do it for me."

And he named her Death.

Death

She stood on one foot
   for fifteen thousand million years.
She ate nothing but air
   for twenty thousand years.
She stood silent in water
   for eight thousand years.
Still, he would not listen.

"But it's what I created you for,"
   Brahma said, using masculine logic.

Death began to weep.

"Everyone will hate me,"
   she said.
"I'm afraid."

So Brahma consoled her;
   he said, "You mustn't be selfish.

"Every tear you shed
   will become a disease
to afflict the earthly creatures.
   They won't blame you then
when their time comes
   but will learn, perhaps,
to long for you.
   Desire and anger
will go as your helpmeets
   and bewilder the mortals
in their final moments."

And so it was
   that Death bowed her head
and accepted her fate.

The Howler

Alone at the center of the world,
the Grandfather sat on a lotus blossom,
practicing the most severe asceticism,
intent on creation.
He wanted a son.

Nothing happened.
He waited and waited.
Anger rose in him
and escaped from his eyes
in two teardrops.
From them,
shadows were born.

The Grandfather looked on what he had done
and despised himself.
Enraged, he stopped his heart.
He released his thoughts
and with a huge sob, let go his life.
And that final breath spewed from him
like a meteor storm, flared up
and congealed.
An awful howling pierced the sky.
Rudra was born.

Brahma,
asleep in the sea,
woke up and cried:
"You! Howler!
Stop that roaring and create!"

So Rudra, the Howler,
turned his thoughts inward.
From his mind poured forth
myriad three-eyed Rudras
with matted hair and blue throats,
fearless and gleeful as himself,

vast armies of immortal Rudras
bearing tridents, ready for battle.

"Stop!" cried Brahma,
seeing such force. "No more
of these dreadful creatures
exempt from death.
Give us mortal ones,
who are born, grow old, and die."

Undaunted, Rudra withdrew.

"My power is ill-spent on such creation,"
he said.
"Continue it yourself."

So Brahma did.

And from that day
the great three-eyed Rudra,
born of flame and rage and wisdom,
was known on earth as Siva,
the Destroyer.

Indifference

Everybody in the world was bored.
   They felt no passion, no grief.
Brahma saw their indifference
   and grew angry.
His anger frothed from him,
   congealing in a huge molten sphere.
It was half man, half woman.

"Divide yourself," Brahma commanded.
   Then he took all that maleness—
passive as pure thought—
   and all that femaleness—
fierce and vital and urgent—
   and shaped it in various forms:
soft, hard, curving, smooth,
   sweet, biting, wicked, pure.
And he scattered all those disparate creatures
   over the earth.

And they mingled
   and clashed;
and the women's vitality pierced
   the men's meditations
as sperm does an egg.
And poetry was born from it.
   And war.

The Milking of Prithvi

King Vena had no children
and when he died
the earth was without a ruler.
Lawless bands roamed the towns
and famine wrung whole continents:
all the people lived in fear.

So the wisemen, the sages
and Brahmins, got together.
They churned the limbs
of the dead king
and brought forth Prithu—
most perfect—incarnation of
Vishnu,
and crowned him king
of all the world.

But Prithvi, the earth goddess,
would not submit to him,
nor yield food for his subjects.
He tried to force her,
but she took the form of a cow
and ran away.
Quick as thought, he caught her
and held her fast.

Trembling,
she begged for kindness.

"My milk has dried up,"
she said.
"I must be suckled properly."

So Prithu bade the world's creatures

come and nurse her,
and she would yield to each
what was theirs.

And when the snakes came,
Prithvi's milk turned
to poison in their throats,
for this was to be
their special gift.

II.

The Great Blue God

The Sari Thief

Above the budding sunrise
and the tumbling murmur of the river,
Krishna sits smiling
in the cleft of a kadamba tree.
The limbs around him sport
a strange, silky foliage—
piles of sun-colored saris
stolen from the bathing milkmaids.

Oh happy god, all-powerful,
he lingers his eyes
on the scene he has created:
a cluster of bare beauties—
some cowering in consternation,
a few not quite so concerned.
Like many supplicants, these girls
have found the thing they most desire,
but, alas!
not in the way they'd imagined.

Poor milkmaids! who have fasted and prayed,
day after day, who have bathed
and scented, and braided their hair,
who have roamed the forest
with yearning hearts, in search
of their god, in hope
of his love, and now—
how he has tricked them!

The gopis want their clothes back.
Hesitant, shy, the girls slip,
one by one, from the sheltering stream.
Black rivers of hair tendrilling

over shivering backs, they gather
before the eyes of god.

Krishna descends and—slowly—
distributes the saris. Solemn-faced,
he delivers a sermon
on modesty.

Devoutly, prettily the girls
raise their arms to him.
"But dearest Krishna!
We bathe here only for love of you."

Such devotion
even a god cannot resist.
Smiling, Krishna makes his promise:

tonight they will find him,
waiting in the forest.

Sporting with the Gopis

The river is lighthearted today
bucking and twisting
like a young goat mad on spring.
Caught up in its mood, waist-deep
in its frolic, the maidens, too,
splash and whirl, cavorting their arms
in some wild dance, casting their eyes
on the great blue god—quick
as the waters, bright as the heavens—
swimming there among them.
Hips drenched in silk, breasts
full to the sun, the milk-maids circle him.

Oh how Krishna loves sporting with the gopis!
Afloat amidst gold-gleaming arms, adrift
in a billowing current of sun-bronzed breasts,
as round as coconuts and sweet,
he feels like a child, he recalls
that he lost his mother
and that

> a demon came to him
> in the enchanting form
> of a woman. (But even then,
> as a baby, Krishna knew
> the world was a dangerous game.)
> He sucked the poisoned milk
> from her teat, and then—
> boy that he was—
> kept on sucking.
> He swallowed her up,
> body and black soul,

and her vile intentions spun off,
a whirlwind into the night.

That was the beginning.

Now Krishna swims with the milk-maids
in a river broad as the sky,
lively with lotus flowers, glistening
with bodies, sweeping along trees,
goats, girls, wind, flowing on
and forever, spilling forth
from this page of time, and,
he, heart full, swells
with desire for the full-breasted
beauty of the world, with gratitude
for the goodness of these gopis.
He imagines how tonight
he will play his flute for them.
He promises himself
he'll make each one blossom.

Krishna's Lament

Madness draws its seven swords;
the violet stars drip down pale poison.
Kamadeva (potent god!)
bewilders me with silver moonlight.

An aching fragrance churns the night—
the fragrance of the night-queen flower.
I've churned a thousand women's hearts
but now I know the pain of longing.

I am a god, yet call on gods:
remove this love that pierces me.
Or let me have one night with her
and I'll beguile her heart away.

Sad-eyed Radha, night-queen goddess,
blossom in this silver night.

Radha's Bath

Surrounded by her women, she
milks the last moisture
from a stormcloud of hair. Fragrant black,
it snakes and nibbles
along her moon-pale back, her thighs,
against skin still cool
from the bath. She sits all absorbed
in grave decisions:
one attendant holds out jewelry,
another her silks.
The colors speak to her; the warm
pearls reflect her heart.

Outside the open pavilion,
afternoon lies hot
against a dark and tangled sky.
The river whispers.
A lone peacock stretches its neck
skyward and cries out.

Each move the lady makes is smooth,
considered; she seems
calm, though her hands tremble. Standing
quietly apart,
her lord, the blue-skinned god Krishna,
watches her prepare:
his thoughts still, his immortal heart
racing.

Painting Radha's Toenails

There is nothing more charming
than a god on his knees;
and Krishna—on his knees—
knows this.

He kneels at Radha's feet
and tenderly rests her sole
in his right hand.
Eyes lowered,
he paints her toenails
crimson as her lips.

A maid appeals to Radha:
acknowledge this honor!
Complacent Radha
leans on one elbow,
rests a hand on the pommel
of her chair; she accedes
the honor to him.

All about them,
afternoon air whispers.
A peach tree rubs its blossoming limbs
against a steady cypress.

Solid, patient,
the kneeling Krishna paints.
Each brushstroke
quickens a little flame.

III.

Night and the River

The Snake Song

A hundred pearls cling
like drops of milk
to her throat, to her wrists;
they drip from her veil
as she sits, pale as milk,
in her stone-smooth tower.
It's dark inside, so dark.

What is it this sad girl
feeds to the snake
as he wends
through the air
like chords of a song,
like a raga through her mind,
as he lifts toward
her hand, as he
levitates
outside her hooded window?

The day is still and flat
and her soul frail and thin
and her eyes slow and sad
as the snake flicks
his tongue toward
the cup in her hand.
She sighs
at the song she hears.

What is it that she offers
in a flared lotus cup,
as her pearls clot and cling
like tears of milk,

as the snake
curves a rhythm
like song through the day,
as the curtain flares smooth
from the tower
of her mind
and she sits
at her window
in the air like silk?
Is it honey?
Is it blood?
Is it milk?

पावसघन अँधियार महि रह्यो भेदन हिद्दान । रातिघोर मन्जोनेपरतलखिवक
वीचकवान ॥ध्र॥

Night and the River

According to legend, chakwa birds can be
together only by day and at night must separate.

The darkness of this monsoon season
never ends.
Day is like night.
The river is black.
Lightning snakes down
from a sadistic sky
to tease the bare earth
as it waits, sighing,
for the ravishing flood.

On a balcony, the lovers sit
protected, in flickering lamplight,
and watch with awe
the storm's fierce pleasure.

Below them, a pair of chakwa birds
stand separated
by the irrational stream.

When Vines Shed Their Leaves

Leaves fall
from the vine
that twines
the tree
like tears
from the eyes
of the pale
lady
who suspends
the hour
of the clinging
dusk
in the sap-sprung
grove
of the
trysting place
where
she shed
her silks
in petaling
drifts
and twined
her complacent
lover.

Majnun, the Mad One

Love tore a hole in his stomach
and all the hope drained out.
And people were like nettles to him,
and words like mosquitos
around his ears.

He went off, far away,
and sat. He sat
day after day
unmoving.
And all the animals
of the forest
drew near him
and stared at him,
silent;
and their blood recognized
his wild and wounded spirit.
And they watched
as the memory of Laila—
beautiful as the night—
picked clean his bones.

Monsoon

Bending to the harsh wind of memory,
caught in a gale erupting from her past,
the woman's mind and heart cannot agree
on where to turn. Her saffron veil, held fast,
billows, begins to tear; she feels the cruel
fingers of shadow bruise along her skin,
unwilling to let go; and every jewel
the woman wears—eternal, cold, akin
to death—weighs on her now like lead, like lies.
Cold horizontal rain begins to cloud
the whiteness of her gown, to sting her eyes
and wrap her figure in its clammy shroud.
No shelter from this private, strange monsoon,
she darkens with it, shadowed like the moon.

The Betrayal

She has waited so long for him
   the night has grown pale.
Her marble terrace stretches
   grey and barren around her
as sky retches the dawn
   like some raw, unwholesome thing.
A peacock strains his beak
   toward her hand.
A single poplar pierces
   the tepid air.

Something has hold of the woman,
   some strange spell.
Pain thickens her throat,
   contracts her chest;
the thought of him
   gnaws her like a disease.
It steals her breath,
   undermines the command
to keep on living,
   crosses her up in a haze
of contradictory impulses:

to breathe, to beat, to be
or not to breathe, beat, be.

The woman feels her pearls burning
   like kisses against her throat.
She tears at them, casts them away.

The Undoing

Her body curves
   in the shape of its wish
      to once more be unborn:

      to step no more
         in the treacherous dance of the gods,
      to chant no more
         the eerie song of the stars,
     to gnaw no more
         the deceitful herb of hope—

      just to cry itself a surrounding sea
      and slowly undo time:

   become a fleshy tendril, an unquickened germ,
   the constant void of desire.

Emerging from the Beast

He fell in
to the belly of the beast
and for three years
remained in darkness.

He beat his head
on the creature's cold ribs.
He clawed and heaved
at its oozing sides.
Fear held him
to her clammy breast,
and the man slept not.

But one day,
the monster yawned;
and the man writhed
from its venomous throat,
emerged to the dreaming world.

And as sun washed over him,
three years dissolved
like salt in the thirsty ocean,
leaving only a taste
of brine in his throat.

IV.

Legends, Icons, and Endings

The Hermit

On the banks of the river Gomati
among wild birds and blossoms,
fruit trees and grazing deer
lived the great hermit, Kandu.

He practiced such fasts,
such vows and restraints
that the gods all looked on
in wonder.

"Aho, what fortitude!
Aho, what extreme tapas,"
they said,
nervous at so much power.

So they sent down a woman
with fragile waist and curving hips,
with glowing face and marvelous breasts,
and all the skills of seduction.

And they sent Love and Springtime
and fragrant Wind along, too,
this Kandu was such an ascetic.

Poor man. Here's what happened:

He saw her on the river bank
and Spring came, out of season.
And the sweet Wind blew and
the cuckoos sang and Love
drew near with his arrows

and struck Kandu with a strange
deep happiness, and goosebumps
rose on his skin. He said,

"Who are you, you fine-hipped,
slim-waisted, adorable girl?
Tell me the truth, lovely brows;
you are stealing my heart."

Then, with the power of his tapas,

Kandu took on the form of a boy
of sixteen years: fine and strong
and suited for all pleasure.

Marveling, the woman thought:
"Aho, the power of tapas!"

And the hermit forgot worship
and study, and prayers and fasts;
he left off meditation and rituals
and welcoming the dawn.

And the beautiful pair made love
day and night.

And every time
she tried to leave,
the lust-filled hermit
detained her.

Then one day, Kandu rose in a hurry
and headed for the river. He shouted,
"The day is ending; I must worship
the twilight."

The woman stared in disbelief.
She said,
"I beg your pardon, sir.
You think it has been one day?

"We've been here sixteen
hundred years, six months
and three days."

Then Kandu saw the truth:
he saw that his wits
had been robbed.

He said, "Fie.
Fie on me. All my tapas lost.
Woman was made to befuddle.
A curse on this shark called lust."

Weapons of the Gods

Imagine being married to the sun!
Samja couldn't bear her husband's brilliance
and ran away to the forest
to live as an ascetic.
She left her handmaid in her place
and the sun begat three children on her
before he noticed the difference.

He looked, then, with his inner eye
and saw Samja as a mare in the forest.
He took the form of a stallion and mounted her,
then brought her home,
promising to temper his brilliance.
He pared off one eighth of his radiance
like a fingernail,
shaved off imperishable light,
which cometed to earth.

And the gods' smith found it there
imbedded, glinting
like the fine edge of intellect.
And he crafted from it
Vishnu's discus, Siva's trident:
the weapons of the gods.

A Hindu Offering

He took the vanquished ruler's gifts—
the elephants, the gold and jewels,
the trunks of silks, the dancing girl—
and told the eunuchs: guard her well.

They took her to the harem's court;
three handmaids bathed and painted her;
they rubbed her skin with fragrant herbs,
burned sandalwood to scent her hair.

They wrapped her form in gauzy silk,
adorned her with a hundred jewels,
put jingling bracelets on her arms
and draped her hips with golden bells.

The Mughal waited greedily,
imagining with dark delight
the undulating dancer's form,
her rolling hips, her rounded thighs.

The eunuchs led the woman in
to where the ruler sprawled reclined.
He pulled the woman close to him
and offered her his cup of wine.

Seductively, she took a sip,
leaned close to whisper in his ear.
A master vanquished by his slave,
the man was lost in fragrant hair.

The woman tipped her amber ring,
poured poison powder in his cup,
pulled back and shyly gazed at him,
pressing the wine-cup to his lip.

Sohni and the Herdsman

In India   a river
Swift and dark
River that divides
River that joins
A man on one side
On the other   a woman

Each night she swims
Swift beauty
Tangled in waves
An earthen pitcher
Clasped to her breast
Filled with the void
Of her lover's days
It lifts her   sustains her
Carries her to him

The cool of night
Moonlight on water
Someone has seen
Her secret journey
Someone has told
Her rigid kin
Someone has taken
Her seared clay vessel
And left her one
Untouched by flame

The woman enters
The ancient river
Heart on fire
Thoughts aflame
Her lover waits
Restless   longing

The shore lies still
Before her   behind her

The woman swims
The endless waters
Swift currents coil
Her trembling limbs
The raw clay vessel
Melts against her
She drowns   and still
The moonlight shines

The Forest Song

The monks are fasting; they kneel and chant;
   the young one rises and slips away.
He skirts the shrine and enters the forest—
   boy like a leaf bud in early spring.

Deer stare in wonder, birds flutter and call;
   sun soothes his face like the hand of a friend.
The path that he follows draws near to the river:
   he hears its seductive murmurs and sighs.

   "I mustn't go on,"
     he hears his mind saying.
   "I won't go back,"
     his young heart replies.

A deep green mango tree shelters above him,
   sheds its sweet fruit along the trail.
The boy stops a moment to lie in its shadow;
   his thoughts whirl and eddy; he closes his eyes.

Light as a deer, a young girl draws near him;
   she's left her goats alone at the stream.
She stares at the boy—pure as a leaf bud—
   "It's Krishna," she whispers, and kneels at his side.

Warm as the sunlight, her hand soothes his cheek.
   Devoutly she kisses the monk's smooth hand.
The boy reaches out—who has lived among hermits—
   and touches her skin, like ripe mango fruit.

His chest begins pounding; his eyes leap open;
   he sees her—round and full and sweet.
The place that his hand lies is close to her heartbeat:
   he feels its seductive murmurs and sighs.

   "I can't go on,"
     he hears his mind saying.
   "I won't go back,"
     his full heart replies.

Unveiling Draupadi

> "Sari madh mai hai ki nari madh sari hai ki
> sari hai ki nari hai, ki sari-hun nari hai."
> —the Mahabharata

Is she a jewel or a golden coin
   that he staked her fate on a throw of dice?
Draupadi was wagered—and lost—by her husband
   to a boorish man from a neighboring tribe.

Drinking and boasting, he dragged her out,
   "I'll show the men what I've won," he cried.
"Take off your clothes," he told the woman.
   Quiet, trembling, Draupadi complied.

Her thoughts flew out to her friend, Lord Krishna.
   "I'll show that barbaric clan," he laughed.
When Draupadi's sari dropped to her feet,
   she was wearing another, still fully clad.

For a quarter hour, she unraveled her saris,
   unwound her sashes, unfurled her veils.
Lord Krishna protected the woman's beauty
   from the wondering men, their evil wiles.

"Is this a woman wearing a sari?
   Or is the sari a part of herself?
Is it a woman who's nothing but sari?
   A woman at all? Or a sari, naught else?"

Ganesha

The elephant-headed Ganesha. Come! Look!
He's such a strange god, sitting on his tiled
altar, serene. He seems to overlook
the dreams of all the world, and cast his mild
gaze over our desires. Yet any child
can understand Ganesha's thoughts. He wants
love, money, honor: all the things we want.

A Village Shrine

For those who understand, who see beyond
mere form, this silver-throated stone, rough-hewn,
with its red-tinged and never-blinking eyes,
is god. Lord Siva incubates within,
his power swelling with every offered flower,
with every humble prayer. And if he rests
on parched earth, or his gaze beclouds with dust,
or paint crumbles in numbing heat, so what?
Perhaps you see only a painted stone.

Durga and the Demon

Durga and the demon
face on the battlefield.
She: radiant, poised.
He: fawning, unctuous.
Each extends a hand in offering.
Both hold back their weapons.
Hers: eight arms resplendent
    with jewels and holy relics.
His: one big sword—
    and a fog of gilded propositions.

The gods gather on the clouded horizon,
avid, aroused.
Durga's lion-mount prances,
delighting in battle.
The moment congeals:
she recites the combat rules.
He sidesteps, stalls,
spews a vapor of enticements.
Draining a silver cup,
Durga evokes a primal frenzy:
arms like raining comets,
she cleaves him, beheads him,
stares at the oozing carcass.

She

When the gods get in serious trouble,
they call for a woman.

When every evil thought swells
and sickens them,
they dream of her;
when their games sprout horns
and haunt them,
they long for her.
When demons dog their heels
and lie waiting in their beds,
the gods run like children
crying to their dark mother

Kali,
who strings the skulls of murdered fools
like oozing pearls about her neck,
whose tongue licks flames across the earth,
who drinks down blood and dines on flesh,
dancing her slow and deathly dance.

And when she comes—
naked, awful—she cleaves
a demonic pile of corpses,
rends arms and legs
and frightful heads. Whipping
the air to a bloody froth,
she comes to take back
what is hers: she
who created this real and unreal world,
who protects it, destroys it,
and plays.